SCARLET VERSES

A COMPILATION OF BOTTLED UP POEMS

MONIKA KARIKALAN

Made with ♥ on the Notion Press Platform
www.notionpress.com

For the moments of doubt and despair.

For the moments of immense joy and love.

For all the men in my life.

Contents

Contents

Contents

Foreword

Once I picked up the verses of Monika Karikalan, I could not put them down until I have feasted upon each and every page of her bottled-up poems. The poetess has captured umpteen emotions and has voiced many muffled sentiments of a mature woman of well-performed thoughts. Starting from her 'prologue', she has kept her word and has not failed to strengthen *the hope of a kinder world.* She has immortalized her 'jovial solitude'. Her 'tasty imperfections' are admirably perfect and are the highest of all forms. One can experience a perfect balance between her 'love and hatred'.

An 'art' has been created by the poetess through her melancholy voice on 'Indian marriages', which absolutely clarifies the life-long commitment well initiated from a *live-stock market.* Then her argument on the existence of a creator shows her rational views that rest upon *choosing and starving.*

The verses travel by its name 'scarlet', very lively, passionate, rich and at times out-busted – 'An agony of joy'.

I am sure that even cupid would enjoy her 'glitch' and will share an umbrella for her 'rain'.

This book of verses speaks volumes and is a must-read for all poetry lovers.

Dr.S.Sumithra

Preface

Life is unpredictable as everyone says. So I thought, why not enjoy this rollercoaster ride calm and composed while holding on to a pen and paper. 'Scarlet Verses' comprises the warmth and woe of this ride. Whenever I cried, whenever I laughed, whenever I loved, whenever I felt numb and whenever I saw someone falling in love, I wrote a poem.

Not only poetry is a way of expressing extreme emotions but a way to convey strong insights. It is so powerful, that it could ignite the emotions we have been burying deep down as we grow up. I'm excited for some of these poems to make you smile and some to make you sob.

Since writing has been a therapy for me, I wish reading will be one for you.

Happy reading!

Acknowledgements

'Scarlet Verses' has been taking form for more than 2 years. Throughout this journey, I met people who truly appreciated this making. Firstly, I would like to thank them all.

Before anything else, I must thank my well-wisher Dr.S.Sumithra, Guest Lecturer, Bharathidasan University for the time she has spent to write a poetic foreword for this book. No words could express my gratitude for the way she incorporated the essence and titles of my poems into an articulate foreword.

I am indeed happy to acknowledge the work of Mr.Amarnath, who gave life to my rough sketches and illustrated them appealingly.

For everyone who criticized me constructively, thanks a lot. You helped this book shape better.

And I am very grateful for the moments of panic and hesitation to express raw emotions through poems and for the moments when I overcame them.

Prologue

I write,

To express the bottled-up warmth and woe,
To expand the idea of equality and freedom,
To strengthen the hope of a kinder world,
To brighten this scarlet red of love and hardship,
To escape this reality of pain,
To make it up for every opinion faded in vain.

Warmth

What would she have written about slow-living and endearment?

1. Breathe in and out

Sit down and do nothing.
Control your thoughts
To control everything.
May your conscience talk to your embodiment!
Through a language
Of universal enchantment.
Listen to the sounds of inhale and exhale;
And paint them in a canvas
With your epitome's quill.
Let the placid disposition remains,
Until there are no regrets to run
Throughout the veins.
Hold the energy between the brows;
To kill the negativity
In your soul's slaughterhouse.

2. Free from thought

Let your heart free from thought;
And go for a walk that will let you to a remedy to your bleeding core which was long confined to four walls of tears, sobs and screams.
Let your heart free from thought;
And pick up a flower you find beautiful to hold it among your thumb and forefinger until you realize that this universe is more beautiful than you have ever imagined.

Let your heart free from thought;
And drop some grains on the terrace for those birds you have no acquaintance with, just to creep in and watch them eat without disturbing their feast.
Let your heart free from thought;
And take a pen to bleed out your soul; not a red one but blue or black on a white sheet since yours is a heart that deserves to be expressed as well as felt by yourself.

3. The Dawn

Golden hour reception,
A silence in the making.
Irony is telling goodnight
To the sunshine.
As sun goes home,
The moon gets back to shift
Still thin and sick,
Of watching lovers underneath.
A cup of cold moonlight,
With extra star toppings,
Let me watch the sky
And pretend to be fine.

4. Books

Am I living far ahead of me
And my own bubble of thoughts,
Not subjected to my own conscience?
Am I bestowed to live
Not one life but a thousand;
Or to wander between
Metaphors and idioms?
Am I prompted to forget

This reality of hurts and neglects,
To forgive myself from the regrets?
Am I in a world of illusions
Or destined to remain there?

5. Immortality

Look into the eyes of eternity,
That is higher above the entire existence
Of human relations.
Forgive the past, forget the future
And also, present if bothers,
As this eternity
Is beyond time and space.
You and I are
A mere flesh of emotions;
Bubbling with joy
And bursting with anger.
Death is the only constant.
So, before the end becomes visible,
Look into the eyes of eternity
And hold hands with serenity.

6. Self-help Book

I used to have a misery diary
Everything they told,
Everything I cried upon
Had been recorded.
It's a self-help book now.

7. Jovial Solitude

I stood there
On the dry yet wet shore;
Alone and happy!
With no fake friends
To judge my appearance and attire,
To tell only what I lack and require.
With no relatives
To question my marital status,
To intrude into my own business.
With no colleagues
To trace my working style,
To deceive me for a while.
With no interfering intimacy
With no lead on love
With no forged fondness
And with no concerns and cares,
I stood there
On the dry yet wet shore;
Alone and happy!

8. The windows to happiness

Open the windows
And welcome the sunshine in.
Place your hand, perhaps with a book and coffee
Where the rays of morning sun fall;
Look at the shadow
Of window bars in them.
Sit there,
Where your face could face the shine,
You'll glow in and out.
Let your fresh wet hair,
Dry with sunlight's company.
For once in your lifetime,
Open the windows!

9. Love of my life

When the entire world seems a stranger,
You understand me so well.
You knew, know and will do,
The needs of every mood.
You hand me over that warmth,
Whenever I reach out;
Better than any hug.
So, I'll take this opportunity
To tell you
That I can't live without you.
My constant forever cup of coffee!

10. Midnight

While nights drill out the embarrassing past,
The mind tries to remember some meagre joy;
Silence reminds you of your lonely fragility
But life never fails to remind its beauty.
You enjoy the melancholia,
For the beauty the window casts on the wall
By borrowing a subtle shine
From the street light.

11. Love and hatred

Let the love be upon,
The bitterness of coffee
Not that of toxic relationships;
Dominance of good power
Not that of chauvinistic men;
Stillness of a library
Not that of loneliness;
Dopamine from a hug
Not that of drugs;

Let the love be upon 'love'
Not 'hatred'.

12. Being himself

He is an amalgamation
Of emotions.
Those are emotions are
Unscathed by compulsion.
A compulsion that
Won't allow him
To be himself.
He lost someone
With whom
He was himself.
Thus, he lost himself.

13. Light in darkness

You are the silent language my ears ask for;
You the warmth my core craves;
You are the name my soul screams;
You are a mother's console!

14. Unwritten poems

I would have written you poems.
Those poems would have made you read 'em time and again,
Until you remember them by each word.
You would have smiled reading them;
You would have cherished them;
But, you would have also wanted
To hold the hand that wrote them.
They would have made you cry
Like a lost child;
They would have pierced your prudence
By reminding you of my absence.
This poetess is capable of taking you beyond stars;
But she doesn't want to.

15. Ideology in crisis

Her feminism was screaming for help,
When he opened the door for her.

16. The toil

Love doesn't come hand-in-hand.
It demands tears and tolerance,
It'll test you to the edge of the slope
Until your soul falls down to pieces.
At least, know the consequences
Of climbing too high,
Of loving too deep.
Going too far is risky,
As the way back may seem tiring.

17. Dark side

Tell me about your dark side;
Let's keep the standards of love aside.
I am too eager to know them;
Trust me, I won't make'em a problem.
I promise to love you wholly;
It's not always about the good face solely.

18. Art

He is Van Gogh's painting!
That I can understand
But can never explain.
Sometimes, *almond blossoms;*
Mostly, *starry night.*
I have reasons
That are embedded in my conscience
And no language could express.
You can't ever understand
Nor encourage how I perceive.
You are a different person,
I am a different soul.

He is an art
I love to dote on.

19. The Weirdo

In a world of luxury and extravagance,
I've been searching comfort in kindness.
In a world of show-offs of what they have,
I've been keeping a secret that is not even mine.
In a world of alcoholics and drug-addicts,
I've been sniffing books.
In a world of thoughts of revenge,
I've been watching karma's dance.
In a world of relationship problems,
I've been crying over romance fiction.
In a world of quotes and philosophy,
I've been writing poems on Instagram.

20. Self-love

They told him to love himself
He loved someone who loved him.
In one way or other,
He got love.

21. Glitch

I write poems at 3 AM in quick notes,
But none sent to you.
A subtle love song as ringtone,
No call from you.
I have a great taste in music,
But can't hand you one of the earphones.
I wonder, 'Is love a glitch?';
Life just hanged in heartbreak mode.
And I haven't updated
Since the last time our eyes met.

22. Rain

Let the love be rain
Not just a drizzle,
A downpour.

23. Tasty imperfection

Sleep past the sound of alarm
Until you feel lazy to lie down.
The awaiting to-do list,
A hundred more deadlines,
And the fright of failure can wait,
For you to taste the imperfect day.
This isn't a race for glory but glee.
It is okay to be held back.
Imperfection is splendor.
Embrace failure as if you love it
But get back and try
Every damn time.
Let them wonder how!

24. What can be?

If love can't be easy, what can be?

25. You

Pen to my poetry
Pigment to my paint
Canvas to my craft
Terms to my thoughts
Silence to my sanity
Joy to my glow!

26. Trophy Wife

He took her hands like a trophy he won
And kissed all over her fingers,
Wishing that one of them will bear a ring someday,
Hoped it to be held out by him
And decided a love until then.

27. The writer

You gifted me a typing machine
But have no idea about it.
I can't confine you in a poem!
Not even few chapters,
Not sure about Collen Hoover's
But my book starts and ends with you;
I am yet to write.

28. Love and peace

Love seeks togetherness
During the toughest times,
To ensure that love stays.
And it takes shapes,
Like art and music;
The strongest shapes
In the toughes times.
People should experience
This strongest version
Of the strongest feeling.
They'll be shattered,
They won't make love a war again.

29. Clowns

Eventually, you'll start smiling
At the way they tremble lying.
Eventually, you'll start enjoying the lies
While knowing the exact truth.
Eventually, you'll start laughing
For that way they fake their existence.
Eventually,
You'll start acknowledging the counterfeit.

30. The Questions

Who are we to judge,
Someone's meaning of love?
Is 'love' subjected to judgement?
Isn't it the ultimate meaning of living
And the destination of all journeys?
If everything we do is not for love,
What the hell are we even doing?

31. The Living

Are we even living,
If not for the sunrises and sunsets?
Are we even living,
If not for the small gestures of love?

32. Revenge

I could turn my trauma into a thousand beautiful things that you could hold close to your heart and envy me for the path I have come across.
I could turn my trauma into art and poetry and you'll never know how much pain is engraved in the paint and paper.
I could turn my trauma into a bouquet of pretty flowers of different colors that could make someone's day.
I could turn my trauma into something impressive and influential that makes me want to thank them every single day.
I could turn my trauma into an inspiring story to tell people.
Why would I revenge?
It's a win.

WOE

What would she have written about all the agony and anarchy?

33. To the walls and windows of my room,

You have seen me smile recollecting the memories I cherish the most.
Have you seen me sob recollecting a little more?
You have seen me smile for the small blessings of my life.
Have you seen me sob for yet smaller unfortunates?
You have seen me smile writing that funny poem on Instagram.
Have you seen me sob writing the poems I posted nowhere?
You have seen me smile to the blue screen of my mobile phone.
Have you seen me sob to my pillow under the blanket?

34. Death

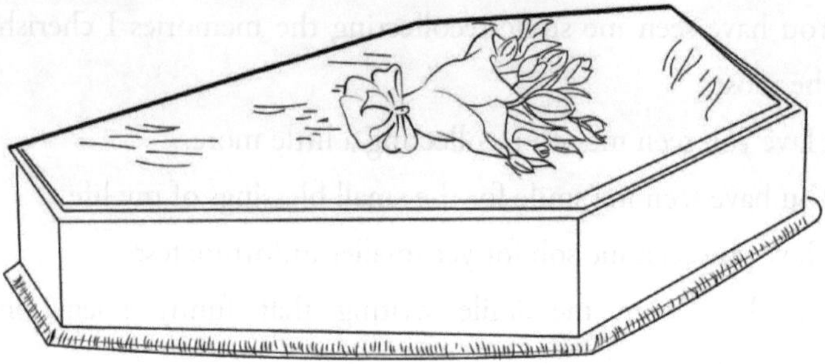

As the coffin smelt of betrayal,
I had to revive
That dead soul of gullibility
And name it 'heart-less'.
Then, I rose from the grave
To everyone's surprise;
But they told me
Aside all the hue and cry,
They told me,
That I have changed.
I rose from the grave,
Not for the first time.
I was never buried;

I was seeded!

35. Empathy

Being not able to express
Is the second worst thing to happen;
Not having someone to understand it
Is first.

36. Heredity

They both grew up in the same home,
Of chaos and tears,
Where the father gives pain
And the mother gives
Tears and forgiveness.
She learnt not to be one
And to choose right;
But he had other ideas.

37. The note

I don't know a single person
Who have written a suicide note
Or one that is capable of.
But I bet there are many.
Why can't we see that person?
We see through them,
Ignoring that story they carry.
I wish I could see that person
Who lost grip of the very last hope;
Who have not one soul to rely on;
Who carries the idea
Of that most dreadful thing.

38. Scars

'Soul' sounds too deep
But too shallow to reach and hurt.
Love reaches fast
Besides, hurts faster,
Just to rip it out,
And give it to you in pieces!
Pieces can be held together,
Scars remain!
Wait with faith
For that right person,
Who'll kiss the scars
And abide the story.

39. Sinners

Aren't you guilty?
For all the injustices you have caused me,
That you were fully aware of.
Aren't you guilty?
For the lies you have told me,
To make sure the key to the cage is lost.
Aren't you guilty?
For the words you have thrown at my face,
Which you knew well would cause me pain.
Aren't you guilty?
For the things you are doing,
Which once you told me were sins.
Perhaps, I would have forgiven,
If only your dictionary has the word 'sorry' in it.
For all the mistakes you have committed,
Shall my love be the punishment!

40. Home

I ran home to you,
To lay my head over
And cry it out;
To complain about a thousand things
And listen to your complaints;
To read you the poems I wrote
And ask you to choose one;
To show you my truths
And still expect love.
I ran home to you,
Just to realize
There never had been a home.

41. Patriarchy

It holds me down
Under the deep blues,
Not letting me breath;
Within a cage that is,
Smaller than my temperament,

Like a shark
Trapped in a fish bowl,
Not letting my existence.

42. Hope

I had a cotton candy hope,
You drowned it with water.

43. Empty hands

That devoid you feel
Where you feel like a giver
And have given them all long ago.

44. Picked up personality

Confined in a world of expectations,
I was never taught to ask,
'What I expect myself to be?';
I was taught about,
'What they expect from me?'.
It was never *what it is*;
It was always *what it supposed to be.*
I picked up this personality,
Since the original version never took a form.
Maybe, she would have been
Braver and wiser;
She would not have cried
Over an argument.

45. Voluntary and forced heartbreaks

Disagreements on one side,
Disgraces on the other.
Abhorrence on one side,
Anarchy on the other.
Contretemps on one side,
Casteism on the other.
Resentment on one side,
Religion on the other.
Hassle on one side,
Honour-killings on the other.

46. The abused and the abuser

If men help women to protect them from men itself,
Why shouldn't they try and help their own mindset?
If he can tell his sister to wear a *dupatta*,
Why can't he wear one over his male gaze?
If a woman knows so many 'abused',
Why doesn't a man know one 'abuser'?

47. Rape

She is in a prison of her own body,
Feels like she doesn't belong there,
Blames herself for someone's wrongs,
That break her serenity into infinite pieces,
That she never knew
How to get them back together.
As if standing in an edge of agony
Where falling would bring death
Staying causes something worse.

48. Misogyny

He had undone the petals from the rose leisurely,
Making her feel the pain of each petal's detachment.

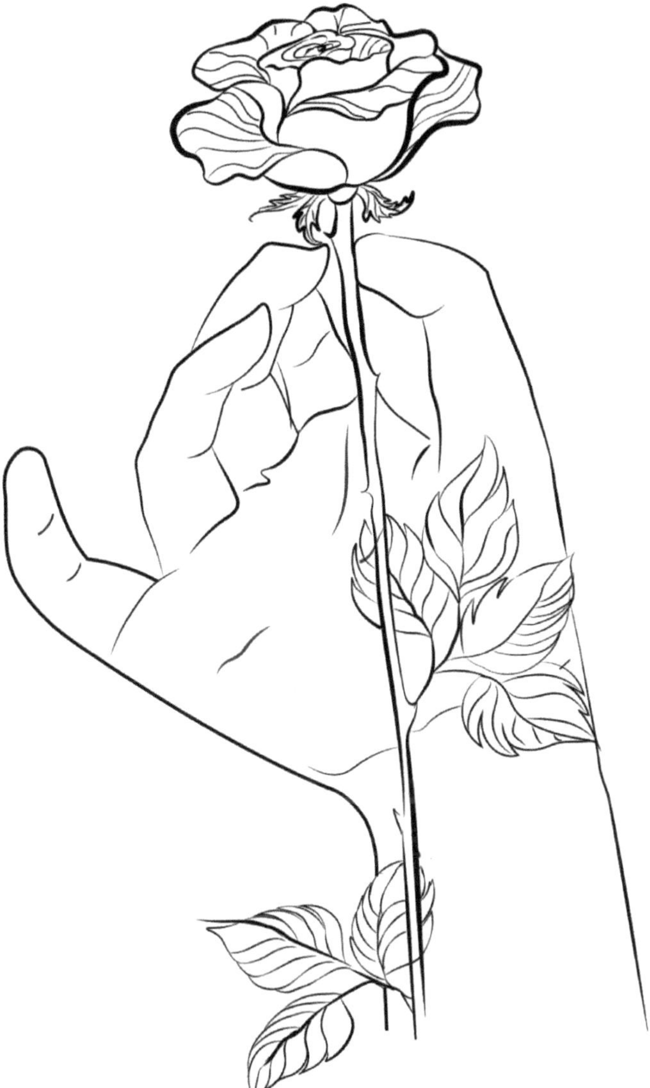

49. Suicide

Do I look like a person
Who would silently write,
How desperately she wants
To kill herself?
Or do I look like a person
Who would write 'stop crying'
Not once but a thousand times
In a piece of paper?

50. God

As far as, there are injustices
In the name of purity,
As long as the greatest of all violences
Happen in the name of religion,
As long as I could remember the name of that child
Who was raped within the compounds of a temple,
As long as one person chooses food
While another dies of hunger,
As long as I could feel the presence of untouchability
In the minds of people,
As long as one half of the human race
Is perceived as reproducing machines,
As long as they ask me to stay away,
Just because I'm bleeding,
How could I trust the existence of a creator?
To the person who once told me very innocently,
'You will believe in God some day',
How could I tell you,
That you'll lose hope?

51. If my daughter makes mistakes,

I'll tell her to make sure whether it is a mistake,
Since they stamp everything a mistake when a girl does it.
I'll tell her not to feel at fault for doing something she likes,
As having dreams and desires is not confined to genders.
I'll tell her that love is the strongest thing in the world.
And that love is for everyone.
I'll tell her about the perverts, abusers, rapists and hypocrites out there.
She'll know them to keep an eye out.
And if she falls prey,
I'll tell her it's never her fault.

52. Man

I won't fall for a man,
Who is a feminist
Only for his girlfriend;
Who gives voice to
the slightest level of
Toxic masculinity;
Who accepts the money
That comes free with the bride
Who adheres to the stereotypes
That are mean and wide.
I won't fall for a man,
Whose father beats his wife
And whose sister fears love.

53. Defective boyfriend

He shows care at intervals
Then goes back to red flags,
Gives love that she craves
Yet, Pull apart right away,
Compliments her body
while dictating her clothing;
Says he likes '*homely girls*',
Fears fellow men,
And has all her passwords.
Girls call him 'protective'
But women know he is 'defective'

54. Pain and power

I have been collecting pain
Which may look light as a feather;
But has all the anguish I am used to suffer.
I have been collecting ‘em,
I have been cherishing ‘em,
While still bearing the bother!
I’ll either evolve or repeat
But never neither.
One day, you’ll see me recast
All the pain into power;
I may reveal the glory
Made of reds and blues of toil.
And that is, my friend,
When you’ll see the real me.
That power I was talking about
Will be love for some
And a lot of misery for others.

55. The secrets

They want her breasts to be enclosed,
Every inch of them;
To be tightened to her body,
Making sure she inhales pain;
Under several fences of clothes,
To be curtained by an extra piece of scarf,
Making them almost disappear,
Faking their non-existence,
As if they aren't supposed be a part.
They do this to one woman,
And then want to know
The secrets of another.
Why struggle
When 'stop staring' could be a better option?
If her breasts could be made invisible,
Why not their thirsts?

56. Mother

She is a captured peacock;
She is unaware of the captivity.
While I was doing everything
To free her from her enclosure,
She had been building one around me;
Obliviously!

57. The Healing

I've realized that,
Before healing others
I should heal myself.
But for healing,
I must know where it hurts.
I was too scared
To look at the wounds.

The scars are bleeding now.

58. Indian Marriages

Welcome to the livestock market!

- Here we offer you decorated commodities that have been taken care for the past 25 years or less.
- You need not pay for the product. Instead, we will pay you for your generosity of buying.
- You'll get free coupons for automobiles, land and jewellery too.
- You can check the beauty standards of the product before buying.
- You can also deny if not satisfied, as the product has got no emotions.
- And if satisfied, you can buy it, for which we will arrange a ceremony.
- This is to tell everybody that we have sold the product successfully and you have bought it effortlessly.

Disclaimer : We are sorry to tell that the product cannot be returned to the seller. But you can destroy the product physically or emotionally as you like.

59. All women

She was touched
In the places she couldn't understand;
She felt as struck in the hold of a monster,
In a dream she could never wake up from,
Like her reflexes are frozen,
In a memory that is constant,
Her screaming makes no sound,
Sufferings are a secret.

She was too young to understand;
Not young enough to forget.
She is every girl.
'Not all men' may be true,
'Yes all women' is the truth.

60. Nevertheless

They gave it a try
To rob me of my voice
By draining the ink from my pen;
As I refilled with blood,
They grabbed my hand.
I couldn't write
I gave blood and flesh
To get rid of the hold.
Could still feel the grip.
Then, they set my papers on fire
And laughed at my failure
Nevertheless,
I brought them back from ashes
To present you my poetry.

9 798889 867074

Printed by Libri Plureos GmbH in Hamburg, Germany